Rehab to Redemption

The Amy Winehouse Story

By

Clara Berg

Copyright © 2023 by Clara Berg. All rights reserved.

This book, "Rehab to Redemption: The Amy Winehouse Story," is the intellectual property of Clara Berg. No part of this publication may be reproduced, distributed, or transmitted in any form or by any means, including photocopying, recording, or other electronic or mechanical methods, without the prior written permission of the author, except for brief quotations embodied in critical reviews and certain other noncommercial uses permitted by copyright law. The author and publisher have made every effort to ensure the accuracy of the information presented but do not assume any liability for errors or omissions.

Disclaimer:

This book, " Rehab to Redemption: The Amy Winehouse Story," is a work of non-fiction that aims to provide a comprehensive and informative account of Amy Winehouse' life. While every effort has been made to ensure the accuracy of the information presented, the author, Clara Berg, and the publisher do not warrant or represent that the contents are free from errors, inaccuracies, or omissions.

Readers are encouraged to conduct their own research and verification to supplement the information provided in this book. The author and publisher disclaim any liability for any loss or damage resulting from reliance on the information contained herein. This book is not intended as professional advice, and any decisions or actions based on its content are at the reader's discretion.

All rights reserved. © 2023 Clara Berg.

Table of Contents:

INTRODUCTION: THE ENIGMATIC AMY	4
CHAPTER ONE: A TROUBLED CHILDHOOD	9
CHAPTER TWO: DISCOVERING THE VOICE	13
CHAPTER THREE: EARLY MUSICAL ENDEAVORS	18
CHAPTER FOUR: FRANK - THE DEBUT ALBUM	23
CHAPTER FIVE: RISING STAR AND CRITICAL ACCLAIM	28
CHAPTER SIX: BACK TO BLACK - A MASTERPIECE EMERGES	33
CHAPTER SEVEN: FAME AND PAPARAZZI	38
CHAPTER EIGHT: LOVE, TURMOIL, AND RELATIONSHIPS	43
CHAPTER NINE: "REHAB" AND BREAKTHROUGH SUCCESS	47
CHAPTER TEN: BATTLING DEMONS - THE STRUGGLES BEGIN	51
CHAPTER ELEVEN: THE IMPACT OF BACK TO BLACK	55
CHAPTER TWELVE: GRAMMY GLORY AND WORLDWIDE TOURS	59
CHAPTER THIRTEEN: BEHIND THE LYRICS - AMY'S SONGWRITING	63

CHAPTER FOURTEEN: A LIFE UNRAVELING   67

CHAPTER FIFTEEN: THE INTERVENTION AND REHAB   71

CHAPTER SIXTEEN: THE TROUBLED RETURN   75

CHAPTER SIXTEEN: THE TROUBLED RETURN   78

CHAPTER EIGHTEEN: LEGACY AND POSTHUMOUS RECOGNITION 82

CHAPTER NINETEEN: AMY'S INFLUENCE ON MUSIC   86

CONCLUSION   90

Introduction: The Enigmatic Amy

In the dimly lit corner of a smoky jazz club in London's Camden Town, the sultry voice of a young woman captivated the audience, leaving them spellbound. As the notes of a melancholic ballad hung in the air, the spotlight revealed a figure with raven hair, smudged eyeliner, and a voice that carried the weight of a thousand sorrows. That was the first time many had the privilege of experiencing the enigma known as Amy Winehouse.

With her distinctive beehive hairdo, retro fashion, and a voice that could pierce your soul, Amy Jade Winehouse was more than a musician; she was an unforgettable force of nature. Born on September 14, 1983, in the vibrant, multicultural neighborhood of Southgate, North London, Amy's story was one of striking contrast and compelling contradictions.

On the surface, she was the embodiment of a bygone era, a timeless siren channeling the spirits of Billie Holiday, Sarah Vaughan, and Dinah Washington. Her deep, smoky voice possessed a raw sensuality that was a rare find in the modern music landscape. She crooned about love, heartbreak, and the dark side of life with a level of authenticity that drew listeners into her turbulent world.

But beneath the surface lay an enigmatic puzzle, a complex soul entangled in a web of personal demons. Amy's life was a tapestry of highs and lows, filled with the brightest musical moments and the darkest personal struggles. Her lyrics were laced with her own battles with addiction, love, and self-destructive tendencies, making her a compelling yet tragic figure.

As we delve into the labyrinthine corridors of Amy Winehouse's existence, we'll unravel the layers of her complexity, one by one. The "Rehab to Redemption" journey takes us from her formative years as a precocious child singing jazz standards to her meteoric rise as a global sensation and, ultimately, her heartbreaking descent into the abyss of addiction.

Her meteoric ascent to fame was propelled by the release of her second album, "Back to Black," which garnered critical acclaim and established her as an international superstar. Songs like "Rehab" and "You Know I'm No Good" became anthems of a generation, and Amy found herself thrust into the unforgiving spotlight of celebrity.

But, as the world adored her talent, Amy grappled with the harsh realities of life. Her tumultuous relationships, tabloid fodder, and a public battle with substance abuse turned her existence into a real-life tragedy played out on the world stage. Friends and family, helpless as they watched her struggle, could only stand by and hope that she'd find her way back to the light.

Through her music, Amy had an extraordinary ability to bare her soul, to communicate her most intimate pain and desires. Her songs were confessions etched in musical notes, detailing the depths of her emotions, turmoil, and desire for redemption. The themes of her work spoke not only to her personal struggles but also to the universal experiences of love, heartbreak, and the quest for identity.

In the course of this biography, we'll journey through the highs and lows of Amy's life, from her tumultuous relationships to her struggles with addiction and the intense creative process that brought forth her timeless music. We'll explore her relentless pursuit of authenticity and how it often led her down a perilous path.

Amy's enigmatic charm lay in her unapologetic honesty, her willingness to lay bare her scars and vulnerabilities through her music. She was an artist who never held back, even when her own life was spiraling out of control. It's this very vulnerability that resonated so deeply with her fans and solidified her place in the pantheon of musical legends.

As we embark on this journey through Amy Winehouse's life, we'll witness her remarkable talent and her harrowing struggles, leading to a poignant exploration of her quest for redemption.

Hers is a story that transcends the bounds of music, and it's a story that deserves to be told, remembered, and celebrated. Amy Winehouse was an enigma, and it's in the depths of her enigma that we find the soul of a remarkable artist, a complex individual, and a human being who left an indelible mark on the world.

Chapter One: A Troubled Childhood

Amy Winehouse's life began in the heart of Southgate, North London, in a home filled with the echoes of jazz and the aroma of home-cooked meals. It was a humble beginning, but one infused with a deep appreciation for music. Lurking beneath the surface of this seemingly ordinary life, however, were the early seeds of an enigma in the making.

Born on September 14, 1983, Amy Jade Winehouse was the product of a unique blend of family heritage. Her father, Mitchell Winehouse, was a cab driver, and her mother, Janis Seaton, worked as a pharmacist. These seemingly conventional professions held a stark contrast to the world she would later inhabit.

Amy's family was steeped in the traditions of jazz, a passion handed down through generations. Her paternal grandmother, Cynthia, had been a singer in the family's own jazz band, and her uncles had carried the torch forward as well. This musical lineage was an essential part of Amy's upbringing, as she was surrounded by the rich melodies of jazz standards from a young age.

Yet, the harmony of her childhood was marred by the dissonance of her parents' tumultuous relationship. The cracks in their marriage soon became fault lines, and by the time Amy was nine, they had separated. This event left a profound impact on the young girl, who often found solace in music. It was through this medium that she began to express the emotions that had been stirred by the instability of her family life.

The backdrop of her early years was far from idyllic. Amy attended Osidge Primary School, where she stood out not just for her musical talents but for her independent spirit. Her classmates fondly remembered her as a force of nature, a girl who wasn't afraid to speak her mind. It was evident even then that she was not cut from the same cloth as her peers.

Despite the challenges that life threw her way, Amy's love for jazz was unwavering. Her father, who recognized her innate musical talent, soon began to teach her guitar chords. In her teenage years, the foundation of her passion for music was laid, and it was not long before she was penning her own songs, the earliest inklings of the artist she would become.

The echoes of her parents' divorce continued to reverberate in her life. As she transitioned to secondary school, Amy's rebellious streak became more pronounced. She experimented with her appearance, adopting a distinctive style that combined elements of vintage fashion with an edge that was uniquely hers. Her iconic beehive hairdo and heavily lined eyes began to take shape, embodying her defiance and individuality.

By the time Amy entered the prestigious Sylvia Young Theatre School at the age of 12, her musical aspirations had begun to overshadow her academic pursuits. This new environment, filled with like-minded peers, nurtured her love for performing. Yet, it was also here that she began to grapple with issues that would later haunt her—bulimia and anorexia. The seeds of her self-destructive tendencies had been sown, growing alongside her musical ambitions.

"Chapter One: A Troubled Childhood" marks the origins of Amy Winehouse's complex journey. It was a time of contradictions, where the love of music clashed with the turbulence of her family life, and the first glimpses of her enigmatic personality began to emerge. As we delve deeper into her story, we'll see how these early experiences and challenges paved the way for her ascent to stardom and the trials she would face along the path to redemption.

This narrative captures the essence of Amy Winehouse's early years, blending the influence of her family's jazz heritage with the challenges she faced in her personal life. It sets the stage for the complexities that would define her future.

Chapter Two: Discovering the Voice

In the annals of musical history, certain artists stand out not just for their vocal prowess but for the profound emotional depth they bring to their songs. Amy Winehouse was undeniably one of these rare gems. Her journey to discovering her extraordinary voice was not just a stroke of fate but a testament to her inherent talent and unwavering dedication to her craft.

As the echoes of her turbulent childhood reverberated through her teenage years, Amy's passion for music became an increasingly essential refuge. The troubled waters of her family life were navigated with the soothing balm of jazz standards and the harmonies of her guitar.

Amy's unique vocal abilities became evident during her early years, and those who had the privilege of hearing her sing in the cozy confines of her home recognized the spark of a prodigy. Her father, Mitchell, encouraged her vocal talents by introducing her to the greats of jazz, from Ella Fitzgerald to Sarah Vaughan. This exposure would prove pivotal in shaping the distinctive qualities of her voice, and Amy's earliest influences would become the pillars of her unique style.

At the age of 14, the momentous occasion arrived when Amy received her first guitar. It was a gift from her grandmother, Cynthia, who had recognized the growing intensity of her musical inclinations. The guitar quickly became an extension of her being, a tool with which she could not only interpret the jazz classics she adored but also craft her own compositions.

Her discovery of the guitar marked the beginning of her songwriting journey. Amy had always been a poet at heart, and now she could channel her poetic expressions into music. Her lyrics, laden with raw emotion and an uncanny understanding of love's complexities, hinted at a depth of experience that far exceeded her tender years.

One of the pivotal moments in her early career came when she was introduced to Simon Fuller, the renowned talent manager who would later guide the Spice Girls and later her career. Her raw talent left an indelible impression, and he would go on to play a crucial role in shaping her career trajectory.

Amy's unique voice wasn't confined to the echoes of her home; she began performing in small local venues, honing her craft and testing the waters of live performance. Her early shows were marked by a combination of vulnerability and fierce determination. It was clear that she had something special, something that would soon take the music world by storm.

Her distinctive style began to take shape during this period. Her fashion choices, a fusion of vintage elegance and street-edge, became an integral part of her identity. The iconic beehive hair, sultry eyeliner, and eclectic wardrobe choices were not just superficial adornments but outward expressions of her inner enigma.

As she delved into the world of jazz and soul, Amy's voice continued to evolve. She possessed a contralto vocal range, a rarity in the world of pop and contemporary music. It was a deep, smoky voice, laden with pathos, capable of conveying the most profound emotions. Her voice was her instrument, and she wielded it with the precision and grace of a virtuoso.

Amy's journey into the music industry was marked by a relentless pursuit of authenticity. She had little interest in conforming to the mainstream pop culture of her time. Her devotion to the old-school jazz and soul genres, and her determination to bring them back into vogue, were unwavering.

It wasn't long before her talent caught the attention of record labels. The prospect of a young woman with such an old soul was intriguing, and Island Records signed her when she was just 18. Her debut album, "Frank," released in 2003, was a testament to her love for jazz and her exceptional songwriting skills. The album was well-received by critics and marked her official entry into the music industry.

In "Chapter Two: Discovering the Voice," we witness the burgeoning of Amy Winehouse's prodigious talent. Her distinctive voice and style were shaped by a profound love for jazz and an unwavering commitment to authenticity. This chapter sets the stage for her ascent in the music industry, a journey marked by remarkable achievements and the complex, often turbulent, facets of her life.

This narrative delves into the early stages of Amy Winehouse's musical journey, focusing on her discovery of her unique voice, influences, and the beginnings of her career. It encapsulates the essence of her authenticity and devotion to jazz and soul, which would become hallmarks of her artistry.

Chapter Three: Early Musical Endeavors

In the grand tapestry of Amy Winehouse's life, the threads of her musical journey began to weave a tale of artistic evolution that transcended time and trends. It was a journey marked by poignant encounters, formative experiences, and the unwavering commitment of a young artist determined to carve her own niche in the world of music.

As Amy's teenage years unfolded, her affinity for music deepened. Her debut as a singer, though humble in scale, carried a significant weight. Her early musical endeavors began in the small venues of North London, where she laid the foundation of her performing career. These intimate spaces became her proving grounds, where she learned to command the stage and enchant the audience with her mesmerizing voice.

The distinctive quality of her performances was not merely the melodious tone of her contralto voice, but her ability to infuse each note with a depth of emotion that resonated with her listeners. At a time when auto-tuned perfection dominated the airwaves, Amy's raw, unfiltered vocals harkened back to the golden age of jazz and soul.

Her appearances in local jazz clubs were marked by an emotional intensity that was rare in a young performer. It was as if she channeled the heartache and longing of the jazz classics she loved so dearly. The audience was transported to a bygone era, where the nuances of heartbreak and desire were laid bare in every note she sang.

Yet, this era of early musical endeavors was not without its challenges. Amy's defiance, often a virtue on the stage, sometimes spilled over into her personal life. Her school years, for instance, saw a tug of war between her love for music and her obligations as a student. The Sylvia Young Theatre School provided her with an ideal platform to nurture her talents, but Amy was not one to conform easily to the rules and routines of academic life.

In hindsight, her obstinacy proved to be a double-edged sword. She was expelled from Sylvia Young due to disciplinary issues, a decision that would alter the course of her life. Amy's expulsion marked a turning point; it was a nod to her unyielding spirit and, simultaneously, a catalyst for her undivided pursuit of music.

The rhythm of her life began to synchronize with the beats of her heart's true calling. Her talents were not limited to singing; she was a songwriter of profound insight. Amy's lyrical compositions were woven from the threads of her own life experiences, replete with love, loss, and the ceaseless quest for identity.

Her songwriting was not a mere artistic exercise but a therapeutic outlet. It was a means of expressing the profound emotions and inner turmoil that had defined her life. Each verse and chorus were a revelation, a confession, and an offering to the world of her unfiltered soul. Her compositions would soon become the cornerstone of her success, transcending mere words and melodies to become profound expressions of the human condition.

The release of her first album, "Frank," in 2003, signaled her official entry into the music industry. It was a showcase of her multifaceted talents, where she not only lent her captivating voice to the songs but also unveiled her remarkable songwriting abilities. The album was received with acclaim and established her as a rising star in the music world.

One standout track, "Stronger Than Me," exemplified her distinctive style. The song was a manifestation of her refusal to conform to clichés and conventions, a rebellion against the prevailing norms of pop music. It was marked by a sassy, unapologetic tone, a harbinger of the authenticity that would become her signature.

In "Chapter Three: Early Musical Endeavors," we delve into the pivotal phase of Amy Winehouse's artistic evolution. Her early experiences in local clubs and her expulsion from Sylvia Young Theatre School set the stage for her unrelenting commitment to music. Her prowess as a songwriter and her debut album "Frank" marked the first steps on her journey toward international stardom, a journey laden with emotional depth and a commitment to authenticity that would define her career.

This chapter illuminates Amy Winehouse's early musical endeavors, highlighting the formation of her distinctive style, her resilience, and her burgeoning career as a singer-songwriter. It captures the essence of her authenticity and the emotional intensity she brought to her performances.

Chapter Four: Frank - The Debut Album

In the realm of artistry, the debut offering of an artist is akin to a painter's first stroke on a blank canvas or a writer's initial word on an empty page. It is the moment when the artist presents themselves to the world, unmasked and vulnerable, exposing the raw essence of their craft. For Amy Winehouse, this seminal moment arrived with the release of her debut album, "Frank." This was the inception, the genesis of her narrative in the annals of music history.

Released in 2003, "Frank" wasn't just a collection of songs; it was a declaration, an artistic manifesto. The title itself was a homage to Frank Sinatra, one of Amy's earliest musical influences, and a nod to the classic era of jazz that had captivated her young heart. It signified her intent to traverse the musical landscape with the same audacity, the same unapologetic honesty, and the same thirst for exploration that marked Sinatra's legendary career.

From the very first track, "Stronger Than Me," it was evident that "Frank" wasn't going to follow the formulaic path of pop music. The song, a candid exploration of gender roles in relationships, was far removed from the sugar-coated love songs that dominated the airwaves. Amy's voice, like an old vinyl record playing in a dimly lit jazz club, carried an emotional depth that was as profound as it was unusual for a debut artist.

The album's lyrics were a window into Amy's soul. Each track was an autobiographical page, candidly narrating her experiences, heartbreaks, frustrations, and desires. "What Is It About Men" was a poignant reflection on her own romantic tribulations, while "You Sent Me Flying" wove a story of farewell and the emotional baggage that often accompanies it. Every word was a confession, every note an unadulterated emotion.

Yet, Amy's gift was not limited to her ability to convey complex emotions through lyrics. It was her voice, an instrument as remarkable as the finest

Stradivarius, that truly set her apart. Her contralto range, rich and smoky, was a throwback to the era of Billie Holiday and Dinah Washington. It was a voice that oozed sensuality, a voice that could traverse the entire spectrum of human emotions, from heart-wrenching sorrow to euphoric joy.

In "Take the Box," Amy's vocals were a cocktail of resignation and determination as she bid farewell to a troubled love. "In My Bed" was a seductive confession of desire set to a sultry melody. Each note was an expression, each line a story, and each track an exploration of the complexities of love and life.

"Moody's Mood for Love," a jazz standard made famous by the likes of King Pleasure and George Benson, was transformed by Amy's distinctive style. She infused it with a depth of feeling that made it her own. It was as if she breathed new life into the familiar notes, turning the song into a timeless classic.

Critics and audiences alike were captivated by Amy's unfiltered authenticity. Her debut album was met with widespread acclaim, and it quickly became apparent that she was not just another newcomer; she was a force to be reckoned with. "Frank" marked a pivotal juncture in her career, a moment when the world stood up and took notice of this prodigious talent.

The success of "Frank" was a testament to the power of genuine self-expression in an industry often dominated by conformity. Amy had not compromised her distinctive style. Instead, she had defiantly forged her own path. Her album, with its fusion of jazz, soul, and R&B, demonstrated that her artistry transcended genres. She was a torchbearer for the revival of classic sounds in contemporary music.

"Frank" catapulted Amy onto the international stage. Her performances began drawing larger audiences, and her unique fashion sense, characterized by the iconic beehive hairstyle and sultry eyeliner, became emblematic of her style. She had transitioned from a rising star to a bona fide sensation.

The critical acclaim that followed the release of "Frank" marked a turning point in her career. The album wasn't just a collection of songs; it was an introduction to an artist who would redefine the boundaries of contemporary music. It was the opening chapter of a story that would be written with ink drawn from her heart, a story that would captivate the world.

"Chapter Four: Frank - The Debut Album" encapsulates the genesis of Amy Winehouse's musical journey. It was a groundbreaking debut that showcased her distinctive style, songwriting prowess, and a voice that was as rare as it was evocative. This chapter marks the inception of her meteoric rise to stardom and her enduring influence on the world of music.

This chapter delves into the significance of Amy Winehouse's debut album "Frank," highlighting its impact on her career and the music industry. It underscores the raw authenticity, unique style, and emotional depth that defined her artistry.

Chapter Five: Rising Star and Critical Acclaim

The world of music is an intricate tapestry, woven with the threads of artistry, innovation, and emotional resonance. It is a world where the ascent to stardom often occurs against a backdrop of intense scrutiny, where talent is exposed to the unforgiving glare of the spotlight. Amy Winehouse was no stranger to this journey, and as her career continued to soar, she found herself ascending into the firmament of musical legend.

With the release of her debut album "Frank," Amy had signaled her arrival as a force to be reckoned with in the music industry. Her unique fusion of jazz, soul, and R&B was a breath of fresh air in an era dominated by cookie-cutter pop. Her voice, smoky and evocative, was a departure from the high-pitched trills that were in vogue. Amy was not merely a singer; she was a storyteller, a poet, and an authentic interpreter of the human experience.

In the wake of her debut, her star began its meteoric ascent. Audiences and critics alike were captivated by her unfiltered authenticity. The depth of her lyrics and the emotional intensity of her performances set her apart from her contemporaries. Each song she sang was a journey, a catharsis, and an exploration of love, loss, and the complexities of life.

Amy's album struck a chord with music enthusiasts and industry insiders. It was celebrated for its courageous departure from the mainstream, its daring exploration of raw emotions, and its embrace of the classic sounds of jazz and soul. "Frank" was not just a collection of songs; it was a manifesto, a testament to the power of self-expression and the authenticity of her artistry.

Her live performances became a must-see event. Audiences were drawn by the enigmatic aura that surrounded her, as well as her genuine, often candid, interactions with her fans. She had a way of making each concert an intimate experience, as if she were confiding her deepest secrets to a friend.

It wasn't long before the critical acclaim bestowed upon "Frank" translated into a widespread recognition of Amy's talent. She was awarded the prestigious Ivor Novello Award for Best Contemporary Song for "Stronger Than Me," an acknowledgment of her songwriting prowess. It was a sign that her unique approach to music was not only resonating with listeners but was also being embraced by her peers.

Amy's success was not limited to the shores of her native England. Her music began to traverse the globe, capturing the hearts of international audiences. Her debut album made its mark in various countries, earning her a devoted global fan base. She was no longer just a rising star; she was a musical phenomenon.

In the world of popular music, stardom often comes hand in hand with the relentless glare of the paparazzi. Amy's distinctive fashion choices, characterized by the iconic beehive hairstyle and sultry eyeliner, had made her a fashion icon. But it was her personal life that garnered intense scrutiny. The tabloids chronicled her relationships, her partying, and her struggles with addiction with relentless fervor. Her life was played out in the public eye, a complex narrative that was open to interpretation and judgment.

Yet, Amy's artistry remained untarnished. Her music was a refuge, a haven where she could lay bare her soul and reveal her deepest vulnerabilities. Her albums were diaries, each page filled with poetic confessions and sonic revelations. It was this unwavering commitment to her craft, even in the face of personal turmoil, that endeared her to her fans and kept the flame of her artistry burning.

As her career continued its upward trajectory, her contributions to the world of music were recognized through numerous awards and accolades. The Grammy Awards, one of the most prestigious honors in the industry, were bestowed upon her. Amy was awarded five Grammys in 2008, including Record of the Year and Song of the Year for "Rehab." It was a moment of vindication, a recognition of her extraordinary talent.

"Chapter Five: Rising Star and Critical Acclaim" paints the portrait of an artist ascending to the pinnacle of musical stardom. Amy's distinctive style, her raw authenticity, and her unwavering commitment to her artistry garnered her critical acclaim and an international fan base. Her journey was a complex one, marked by both acclaim and personal challenges, but her music remained a testament to her enduring talent and her profound connection with her audience.

This chapter delves into Amy Winehouse's rise as a musical sensation, highlighting her unique style, emotional authenticity, and international success. It explores the critical acclaim she received and the challenges she faced as her career continued to soar.

Chapter Six: Back to Black - A Masterpiece Emerges

In the realm of music, there are those extraordinary moments when an artist breaks free from the ordinary and leaves an indelible mark on the world. Amy Winehouse's second studio album, "Back to Black," was one of those magical moments. It wasn't just another album; it was a masterpiece, a work of art that captured the very essence of her musical journey.

In 2006, when "Back to Black" was released, it marked a profound shift from her debut, "Frank." It was a musical transformation that would redefine the contemporary music landscape. Amy, like a musical chameleon, had undergone a stunning evolution. The jazzy rhythms of her earlier work gave way to a soulful and vintage sound. The album paid homage to the Motown and girl group sound of the 1960s, a genre that had left an indelible mark on her musical sensibilities.

The title track, "Back to Black," was a gut-wrenching ballad about lost love. It was a song that poured raw emotion, a signature of Amy's artistry. It wasn't just a breakup song; it was a vulnerable confession of heartache. Her voice, as always, was the emotional channel through which she conveyed her deep sorrow. It was a voice that could touch the soul, making you feel her pain as if it were your own.

The album's lyrics were a tapestry of heartbreak, addiction, and the challenges of fame. "Rehab," one of the album's standout tracks, was Amy's sardonic response to her own battles with addiction and the pressures of the music industry. It was a bold statement, a refusal to conform to the expectations of others. Amy's defiance shone through, and her resilience was unwavering.

The album's production, under the guidance of Mark Ronson, was a beautiful fusion of old-school sounds and contemporary sensibilities. The music was like a time machine, transporting listeners to an era of soulful ballads and melancholic melodies. The use of brass instruments, especially the saxophone, added an authentic touch, reminiscent of the golden age of soul.

Amy's songwriting remained at the heart of her artistry. Each track was a heartfelt confession, a profound exploration of the human experience. "Love Is a Losing Game" was a poignant ballad that laid bare the pain of lost love. It felt as if Amy had delved deep into her soul and pulled out the essence of heartbreak.

The critical acclaim that followed the release of "Back to Black" was a crescendo of recognition. It was an album that resonated with audiences and critics worldwide. Amy's story, marked by personal struggles and an unwavering commitment to authenticity, resonated deeply with listeners. It was a tale of redemption through art, a story of transformation and resilience.

The album garnered a multitude of awards, including five Grammy Awards. It was a moment of vindication, a recognition of her exceptional talent. Her songs, often drawn from her own life, became anthems for those facing similar challenges. Amy's unfiltered storytelling had the power to make people feel less alone in their own battles.

However, "Back to Black" was not without its complexities. The depth of emotion that Amy poured into her music often mirrored her own struggles. Her battle with addiction, particularly with drugs and alcohol, intensified during this period, and the album's lyrics offered a mirror into her tumultuous personal life. It was a paradox of art and agony, where her remarkable talent, which had brought her fame, also fueled her inner demons.

The spotlight, once a beacon of her success, became a relentless glare. Tabloids relentlessly documented her personal struggles, and the public eye scrutinized her every move and her battles with addiction. The album's prophetic title, "Back to Black," symbolized her life's trajectory.

"Chapter Six: Back to Black - A Masterpiece Emerges" provides a glimpse into the creation and impact of Amy Winehouse's album "Back to Black."

It celebrates the transformation in her sound, the emotional depth of her music, and the critical acclaim that this iconic work received. It also explores the paradox of her artistry and personal struggles, a theme that would continue to define her career and life.

Chapter Seven: Fame and Paparazzi

The road to stardom is often fraught with unexpected turns and steep inclines. For Amy Winehouse, the ascent to fame was meteoric, but with it came a blinding, relentless spotlight that exposed every facet of her life. Fame, as it unfolded for Amy, was a double-edged sword, and the paparazzi became both chroniclers and tormentors of her journey.

As "Back to Black" continued to scale the charts and earn critical acclaim, Amy's fame spread like wildfire. She had transitioned from being a celebrated artist to an international sensation. Her signature beehive hairstyle and distinctive eyeliner became iconic, emulated by fans and imitated by the fashion world. She was no longer just a singer; she was a style icon.

Amy's live performances were eagerly anticipated events, and audiences flocked to witness the magic of her soulful voice in person. Her concerts were intimate affairs, where it felt as though she was confiding her innermost thoughts to her fans. She had an uncanny ability to create a personal connection with her audience, to make each performance feel like a private conversation.

However, as her star continued to rise, so did the intensity of the paparazzi's pursuit. The tabloids, always hungry for a headline, turned their attention to every aspect of Amy's life. Her relationships, her public appearances, and her struggles with addiction were all fair game. The paparazzi lenses became inescapable, capturing every triumph and tragedy.

The paparazzi's relentless pursuit of Amy took a toll on her mental and emotional well-being. The invasion of her privacy became a constant source of stress. It was as if she could never truly escape the spotlight, even in her most vulnerable moments. The world watched as her personal battles unfolded in the public eye, a cruel and unrelenting spectacle.

The media's fixation on her personal life, particularly her struggles with addiction, was unrelenting. "Rehab," her sardonic response to the pressures to seek treatment, became an anthem that fueled the tabloids' scrutiny. It was as though they were locked in a relentless battle to document her descent, a descent that was played out in headlines and sensationalized stories.

Amy's battles with substance abuse became a central narrative in her public image. The paparazzi's lenses were often there to capture the moments of her most profound vulnerability. The world watched as she grappled with her demons, a struggle that played out in stark and unvarnished images. It was a troubling, painful spectacle that only served to amplify her personal anguish.

The intense scrutiny of her life led to a growing feeling of isolation. Amy felt trapped in a gilded cage, her fame a double-edged sword that granted her success but denied her the privacy and peace she so desperately needed. The burden of being in the public eye was a weight she bore every day, a weight that became increasingly heavy.

Yet, throughout it all, Amy's artistry remained her refuge. Her music was an unfiltered expression of her pain, her hopes, and her experiences. It was an intimate connection with her audience, a lifeline to those who found solace in her lyrics and melodies. Her concerts became a sanctuary, a place where she could share her truth and feel the unconditional support of her fans.

As "Back to Black" continued to make its mark in the world of music, Amy's fame seemed insurmountable. Her performances were legendary, her songs anthems of a generation, and her fashion sense influential. But as her fame soared, her personal life continued to spiral into chaos.

"Chapter Seven: Fame and Paparazzi" unveils the complex relationship between Amy Winehouse and the media's unrelenting attention. It was a chapter in her life where the price of fame became starkly evident. The paparazzi's lenses invaded her privacy and amplified her struggles, creating a narrative that often overshadowed her remarkable talent. In the midst of her fame, Amy grappled with a relentless spotlight, a spotlight that would become both her stage and her burden.

Chapter Eight: Love, Turmoil, and Relationships

In the intricate mosaic of Amy Winehouse's life, the threads of love and relationships were woven with profound intricacy and depth. As her career continued its meteoric ascent in the world of music, her personal life took center stage, characterized by intense passion and undeniable turmoil. The relationships she forged and the love affairs that blazed with the intensity of a shooting star would become defining elements of her story.

One of the most captivating love stories in Amy's life was her whirlwind romance with Blake Fielder-Civil. Their connection was electric, a force of nature that defied convention and swept them both into a tempestuous journey. Their love was a fusion of fiery passion and recklessness, a rollercoaster ride that mirrored the turbulence of their individual lives.

Amy and Blake's relationship was punctuated by unbridled passion, yet it was marred by the specter of addiction. Their shared struggles with substance abuse cast a long shadow over their love story. The ever-present paparazzi, whose fascination with Amy's personal life knew no bounds, chronicled their every move, capturing the moments of both ecstasy and agony.

Their turbulent love story unfolded on the grand stage of public scrutiny. Headlines chronicled their intense highs and devastating lows, turning the pages of their love story into a gripping drama for the world to watch. Amy's music, a reflection of her own life experiences, became a mirror through which the world glimpsed the complexities of her emotions. In "Tears Dry on Their Own," she bared her soul about heartache and betrayal, while "You Know I'm No Good" was a candid confession of infidelity.

As their relationship evolved, Amy's personal battles with addiction escalated, and the strains of fame, coupled with the relentless gaze of the paparazzi, took a toll on their love. The couple's separation and eventual divorce marked one of the most painful chapters in Amy's life. Her heartbreak and turmoil became tabloid fodder, further adding to the complexity of her public image.

Amid the tumult of her relationship with Blake, Amy's music continued to flourish. Her album "Back to Black" stood as a testament to her remarkable ability to channel her personal experiences into her art. Each song on the album was a chapter in her love story, a vivid brushstroke on the canvas of her emotions. It was her way of coping with the intricacies of love, celebrating the joys, and mourning the heartaches.

Amy's relationships weren't limited to her personal life alone. Her deep connection with her audience was profound, transcending the boundaries of the stage. Her live performances were a testament to the depth of her connection with her fans. It was as though each concert was a shared experience, a moment of profound intimacy between the artist and her audience.

However, fame, as it so often does, exacted a heavy price. The paparazzi's unrelenting pursuit of her personal life continued to intensify. Amy's every move, her relationships, her struggles—all were documented in detail, dissected by the ever-watchful eye of the media. Her love affairs, both personal and with her audience, became a central narrative in the story of her life.

"Chapter Eight: Love, Turmoil, and Relationships" delves deep into the personal life of Amy Winehouse, revealing the intricate complexities of love and the profound turmoil that marked her relationships. It's a chapter where passion and addiction danced together, where the ecstasy of love was often followed by the agony of heartbreak. Amy's narrative wasn't confined to the stage; it was an unfiltered exploration of the human condition, a journey marked by both ecstasy and agony.

Chapter Nine: "Rehab" and Breakthrough Success

Amid the tumultuous narrative of Amy Winehouse's life and career, there emerged a singular song that would transcend music to encapsulate her essence, her defiance, and her undeniable talent. "Rehab," the lead single from her remarkable sophomore album "Back to Black," would not merely become an anthem of personal rebellion but a pivotal moment in her extraordinary musical journey.

Unveiled to the world in 2006, "Rehab" was not just a song; it was a bold statement, a candid revelation of Amy's personal battles with addiction and her resolute refusal to conform to the dictates of others. Its very title was an audacious declaration, a sardonic response to the pressure imposed upon her to seek treatment.

The song's lyrics bore an autobiographical weight, offering a raw and unvarnished window into Amy's own struggles. "They tried to make me go to rehab, and I said no, no, no," she sang, her voice dripping with defiance and a touch of rebellion. These words were an unapologetic rejection of the demands of an industry that often sought to mold its artists to fit a particular image.

"Rehab" transcended the realm of music to become a cultural touchstone. It resonated deeply with audiences who had faced their own battles with addiction, elevating Amy to a relatable figure in a world frequently dominated by unattainable ideals. Her unfiltered storytelling created a profound sense of shared experience, uniting listeners in the belief that they were not alone in their struggles.

The critical acclaim that "Rehab" garnered was nothing short of a crescendo, reflecting its impact and significance. It was a song that captured the very essence of Amy's artistry, her unique talent for transmuting her personal turmoil into music that struck at the core of human emotion. The song was celebrated for its unvarnished honesty and its fearless rejection of conformity.

Yet "Rehab" was not confined to the realm of critical acclaim alone. It ascended to the zenith of music charts, becoming a chart-topping sensation and securing Amy her first Grammy Award. This success was a testament to her transformative sound, which deftly combined vintage soul with contemporary sensibilities. "Rehab" marked her breakthrough into the international music scene, catapulting her to newfound fame.

The acclaim and success of "Rehab" served to amplify Amy's star, and the song's iconic video, featuring her signature beehive hair and bold eyeliner, became emblematic of her unique style. She had transcended the realm of being just a musician; she was now a cultural icon—a fearless artist who defied conventions and shattered stereotypes.

However, even as her fame continued to soar, Amy's personal struggles with addiction persisted. The relentless pressures of the music industry, the ceaseless scrutiny of the paparazzi, and the demands of her personal life weighed heavily on her. Her music, while a source of catharsis and creativity, also bore the heavy burden of her personal turmoil. It was a paradox where art and agony were intertwined, and her remarkable talent served as both a lifeline and a tether to her inner demons.

"Chapter Nine: 'Rehab' and Breakthrough Success" delves deeply into the profound significance of Amy Winehouse's iconic song "Rehab." It was a musical milestone that not only marked her breakthrough in the music industry but also encapsulated her defiance and unapologetic artistry. The chapter meticulously explores the autobiographical lyrics of the song and its profound impact on her listeners, showcasing her enduring ability to connect with the shared human experience. It is a testament to her extraordinary journey through music and life.

Chapter Ten: Battling Demons - The Struggles Begin

In the rich tapestry of Amy Winehouse's life, this chapter looms as a pivotal turning point. It is a chapter characterized by the emergence of profound struggles and the relentless battle with personal demons that would come to define her narrative. Her ascent to fame had been meteoric, but beneath its glittering surface, a tempest of turmoil brewed, threatening to engulf her.

As "Rehab" continued to echo through the airwaves, Amy's personal life became increasingly convoluted. The pressures of fame, the ceaseless gaze of the paparazzi, and the intoxicating allure of the music industry created a perfect storm. For Amy, it was a storm of addiction that raged unchecked, its turbulent waves threatening to submerge her in their depths.

Amy's struggles with substance abuse, particularly with alcohol and drugs, now took center stage in her life. The pain and chaos that often accompany addiction played out in stark contrast to her undeniable talent and burgeoning success. It was a paradox of staggering dimensions, where her artistry soared even as her personal life spiraled into darkness.

The tabloids, whose relentless coverage of Amy's life had become a relentless drumbeat, now chronicled her struggles with a disconcerting intensity. The paparazzi's lenses captured moments of vulnerability and her attempts at self-medication. Her journey through addiction was played out in stark, heart-wrenching images, amplifying her personal anguish.

While "Back to Black" continued to be celebrated and played on the world stage, Amy found herself locked in a fierce battle. It was a battle for her own well-being, a struggle to regain control over her life. The words of her songs, which had resonated so deeply with her audience, now took on an even more personal significance. Her music was not just an artistic expression but a lifeline.

The very stage where Amy had once been an undeniable force now became a battleground where she wrestled with her inner demons. Her live performances, once a source of catharsis, now bore the weight of her personal turmoil. Her fans, who had always been a source of support, now watched with concern and empathy, as the artist they loved grappled with her inner struggles.

The battle was not merely against addiction but against a relentless and unforgiving industry. The pressures of fame, the expectation to maintain a certain image, and the demands of a rigorous schedule were unrelenting. Amy, who had always been uncompromising in her artistry, now faced a world that demanded conformity.

However, in the midst of the turmoil, Amy's artistry remained a testament to her enduring talent. Her songs, often drawn from her own life, were powerful confessions of her struggles. "Love Is a Losing Game" was a poignant ballad that laid bare the pain of lost love, while "Addicted" offered an unfiltered look at her own relationship with substance abuse.

"Chapter Ten: Battling Demons - The Struggles Begin" is a heart-wrenching chapter in the story of Amy Winehouse. It unveils the onset of her profound struggles with addiction and the unrelenting battle with personal demons. Her journey through fame, addiction, and the pressures of the music industry takes center stage, leading to a tumultuous and agonizing period in her life. It's a chapter that epitomizes the complexity of her narrative, where artistry and addiction intertwine in a fierce and relentless battle. The dichotomy of her extraordinary talent and personal turmoil is revealed in all its poignant and gut-wrenching detail.

Chapter Eleven: The Impact of Back to Black

In the chronicles of musical history, certain albums have transcended mere notes and lyrics to etch themselves into the collective soul of society. Amy Winehouse's "Back to Black" is one of these remarkable creations. Its release in 2006 ignited a cultural and musical revolution, and this chapter ventures into the profound impact of an album that not only crowned Amy as a musical luminary but also unveiled the depths of her artistry.

When "Back to Black" graced the airwaves, it defied categorization. The album was a brilliant amalgamation of vintage soul, R&B, and a contemporary sensibility that propelled it into the hallowed halls of timeless classics. Each track on the album was a raw outpouring of Amy's life experiences, from the dizzying peaks to the cavernous troughs.

Critical acclaim rained upon "Back to Black" like a monsoon of praise. Music critics the world over were enraptured by its artistry, its authenticity, and the haunting resonance of Amy's voice. Her album raised the bar for soulful, confessional songwriting, and her voice emerged as a beacon of raw emotion that cast a spell over all who listened.

But it wasn't just the critics who bowed before this sonic masterpiece. Audiences across the globe embraced the album with an ardor that spoke to its universal appeal. Amy's songs resonated on a profound level, touching the heartstrings of those who had loved and lost, who had navigated the tempestuous sea of human emotions. Tracks like "Back to Black" and "Love Is a Losing Game" became anthems for a generation that found solace in their haunting melodies and painfully honest lyrics.

However, the impact of "Back to Black" extended far beyond the world of music. It transcended to become a cultural phenomenon. Amy's distinctive style, with her iconic beehive hair, winged eyeliner, and retro attire, became an emblem of cool elegance. Her influence on fashion and beauty was undeniable, forging trends and styles that would continue to endure.

For Amy, this album was more than a collection of melodies; it was the cathartic release of emotions that had long been confined within. Each song was an unvarnished reflection of her life, from the raw defiance of "Rehab" to the unfiltered confession of "You Know I'm No Good," and the soul-baring "Tears Dry on Their Own," which revealed the scars of heartache.

The success of "Back to Black" wasn't just a career milestone for Amy; it was a gateway to a realm of unprecedented fame and scrutiny. Her personal struggles, exacerbated by her newfound celebrity, cast a long and looming shadow over her life. The paparazzi, relentless in their pursuit of every facet of her existence, now bore down with even greater intensity, subjecting her to a ceaseless and unforgiving spotlight.

"Chapter Eleven: The Impact of Back to Black" peels back the layers of Amy Winehouse's legacy. It reveals the critical acclaim and universal resonance of an album that was more than just music—it was a cultural touchstone. The chapter explores how "Back to Black" not only elevated Amy to the pantheon of musical greats but also had a profound influence on the realms of fashion and style. Yet, it doesn't shy away from the personal struggles that simmered beneath the surface, intensifying under the relentless gaze of the paparazzi. Amy's brilliance shone amidst her personal turmoil, and this chapter is a testament to that compelling duality.

Chapter Twelve: Grammy Glory and Worldwide Tours

The chapter of Amy Winehouse's life that unfolded following the release of "Back to Black" can best be described as a whirlwind. The album, a tour de force of artistry and raw emotion, had not only established her as a formidable musical talent but also positioned her in the dazzling spotlight of worldwide fame. "Back to Black" wasn't just a collection of songs; it was a game-changer.

Amy's talents had been unearthed, dusted off, and thrust onto the grand stage. In the wake of the album's critical acclaim, the world beckoned her with open arms. But Amy, as ever, was a complex figure. Her music was the beacon that illuminated her path, but it was also the heavy anchor that kept her bound to her inner demons.

The pinnacle of Amy's post-"Back to Black" journey arrived in the form of five Grammy Awards in 2008. The world watched in awe as she claimed trophies for Record of the Year, Song of the Year, and Best New Artist, among others. She was no longer just an artist; she was a phenomenon. Amy's performance via satellite from London was a defining Grammy moment. Her voice, a raw torrent of emotion, held the audience spellbound. She was unfiltered, unadulterated, and undeniably brilliant.

Yet, despite the accolades and triumph, the bright lights of success couldn't banish her inner shadows. Her tumultuous relationship with Blake Fielder-Civil, her tumultuous ex-husband, continued to be the epicenter of her personal turmoil. Their on-again, off-again saga was a headline-grabbing spectacle that the media feasted upon.

The worldwide tours that followed "Back to Black" were both a testament to her meteoric rise and a stark reflection of her inner struggles. The stage, once a sanctuary for her raw talent and unvarnished storytelling, became a battleground. The pressures of touring, combined with the unforgiving glare of the paparazzi, were unrelenting.

The tours took Amy across continents, from Europe to the United States to distant shores. Her performances were often powerful, raw, and filled with emotion, resonating deeply with her fans. But they were also punctuated by erratic moments, often attributed to the internal demons that continued to haunt her.

Her stage presence was magnetic. Her signature beehive hair and bold eyeliner became emblematic of her style. The audience hung on to every word, every note, and every expression, knowing they were in the presence of an unparalleled talent.

However, the toll of fame, addiction, and personal struggles weighed heavily. The paparazzi, like relentless vultures, documented her every move, capturing her moments of vulnerability, her highs, and her lows. Amy's life was a public spectacle, a rollercoaster ride for all to see.

"Chapter Twelve: Grammy Glory and Worldwide Tours" is a testament to the astonishing highs and abyssal lows of Amy Winehouse's post-"Back to

Black" journey. It unravels the global recognition she received with her Grammy triumphs and the impact her music had on audiences worldwide. Yet, it also confronts the inner turmoil that continued to overshadow her fame, as the tempestuous relationship with Blake Fielder-Civil, worldwide tours, and the unrelenting paparazzi scrutiny became defining features of her narrative. It's a chapter that paints a poignant portrait of an artist whose brilliance was undiminished, even in the face of personal turmoil and relentless scrutiny.

Chapter Thirteen: Behind the Lyrics - Amy's Songwriting

To truly grasp the essence of Amy Winehouse, one must embark on a journey into the very heart of her artistry, into the world of her songwriting. Beyond the signature beehive hair and the smudged eyeliner, there resided a lyricist of unparalleled depth and unbridled candor. This chapter serves as an intimate exploration, a rare glimpse behind the curtain, offering profound insight into the soul of a songwriter whose words were not just lyrics, but the very essence of her being.

Amy Winehouse's songwriting was a revelation, a conduit for her emotions, and an unfiltered window into the tumultuous landscape of her life. Her lyrics were more than mere words; they were her confessions, her stories, and her truths, etched onto the very fabric of her songs. Each line was a mirror reflecting her joys, pains, loves, and anguishes.

"Rehab," arguably one of her most iconic songs, was far more than a catchy tune. It was an unapologetic declaration of independence, an autobiographical account of her unwavering refusal to conform to external pressures. "They tried to make me go to rehab, and I said no, no, no." These words were a fierce assertion of self, a defiance against the industry's attempts to mold her into something she was not. In "Rehab," Amy wasn't just singing; she was laying her life bare.

"You Know I'm No Good," another lyrical gem, was an intimate confession of infidelity and guilt. "I told ya I was trouble, you know that I'm no good." Here, Amy became the unflinching narrator of her own transgressions, allowing her audience to peer into her world of imperfect relationships and emotional complexities.

The title track of her second album, "Back to Black," was a haunting ballad that delved into the abyss of heartbreak and loss. "We only said goodbye with words; I died a hundred times. You go back to her, and I go back to black." These lyrics were an emotional excavation, laying bare the pain of parting and the enduring scars it leaves behind. In her songs, Amy wasn't merely singing; she was baring her soul.

Amy's songwriting wasn't just a skill; it was an extraordinary gift. Her words possessed the rare power to unravel the complexities of human emotions and relationships, making them universally relatable. Her storytelling was candid, unembellished, and brutally honest.

Her ability to draw from her own life experiences and lay them bare in her songs was both her strength and her vulnerability. In tracks like "Love Is a Losing Game" and "Wake Up Alone," she didn't merely create poetic musings; she channeled the echoes of her own joys and sorrows into her lyrics

Yet, beneath the lyrical brilliance was the stark reality of her personal struggles. Her battles with addiction and tumultuous relationships weren't just themes in her songs; they were the crucibles of her life. The love, pain, and turmoil that threaded through her lyrics were not mere metaphors; they were the very fabric of her existence.

Songwriting was Amy's sanctuary, a place where she could confront her demons and exorcise her emotions. Her creative process was often intense, a conduit for her inner turmoil. While it was a source of catharsis, it was also a reflection of her fragile state, a lyrical tightrope walk between brilliance and vulnerability.

"Chapter Thirteen: Behind the Lyrics - Amy's Songwriting" invites you to step beyond the curtain and into the world of Amy's songwriting. It unveils the extraordinary power of her lyrics, which were not just words on paper, but intimate confessions of her life's journey. The chapter delves deeply into some of her most iconic songs, unraveling the profound emotions, experiences, and undeniable truths they held. It's a journey into the very soul of a songwriter whose words continue to resonate with audiences worldwide, transcending the boundaries of time and culture.

Chapter Fourteen: A Life Unraveling

The saga of Amy Winehouse is a tapestry woven with intricate threads of music, fame, and personal struggle. As her career skyrocketed, her personal life embarked on a turbulent descent into chaos. This chapter delves into the tumultuous period when Amy's life began to unravel, and the world watched in a mix of concern and fascination.

In the years following her meteoric success with "Back to Black" and her Grammy triumphs, Amy found herself caught in a whirlwind of pressures, vices, and personal tumult. The music industry's unrelenting demands coupled with her own internal battles created a perfect storm, threatening to extinguish the very brilliance that had propelled her to stardom.

The world had marveled at her distinctive voice and raw songwriting, but it was the relentless scrutiny of the paparazzi that often defined her narrative. Every misstep, every moment of vulnerability was captured and splashed across tabloids. Amy's life had become an open book, her personal struggles exposed for all to see.

Her marriage to Blake Fielder-Civil, a relationship marked by its tumultuous ups and downs, had long been a fixture in the public eye. Their passionate yet toxic connection was a source of endless fascination. For Amy, it was a rollercoaster ride of emotions, punctuated by the euphoria of love and the depths of despair.

The struggles with addiction, particularly alcohol and drugs, were a relentless companion during this period. Amy's personal turmoil played out in stark contrast to her undeniable talent. It was a paradox that tugged at the heartstrings of those who had fallen in love with her music.

The stage, which had once been her sanctuary, became a battleground where Amy wrestled with her inner demons. Her live performances, characterized by their raw intensity and candid emotion, were often marked by erratic moments. The audience, a mix of ardent fans and concerned onlookers, watched with a mixture of admiration and worry.

Amidst the chaos, her music remained her anchor. The songs she created were not just artistry but her lifeline, a means to confront her own pain and turmoil. She bared her soul through her lyrics, offering an unfiltered glimpse into her personal journey.

"Back to Black," the album that had catapulted her to international stardom, was both a blessing and a curse. It had brought her unparalleled recognition and acclaim, but it had also intensified the demands and pressures that came with fame. The album, which was a reflection of her own heartache and loss, became both a solace and a reminder of her struggles.

Amy's fashion sense, with her iconic beehive hair and winged eyeliner, continued to influence trends and styles. Her distinctive look was emblematic of her unique persona, a mix of vintage elegance and contemporary edge.

"Chapter Fourteen: A Life Unraveling" exposes the turbulence that marked this chapter of Amy Winehouse's life. It unravels the pressures of fame, the relentless gaze of the paparazzi, and the internal battles that waged within her. Her tumultuous relationship with Blake Fielder-Civil, the escalating struggles with addiction, and the stage as both a sanctuary and a battleground are all part of this gripping narrative. Through it all, Amy's music remained her constant companion, a testament to her enduring brilliance amidst personal turmoil.

Chapter Fifteen: The Intervention and Rehab

In the tumultuous narrative of Amy Winehouse's life, there emerged a pivotal moment—a beacon of hope amidst the chaos—the intervention. It was an act born of love and desperation; a lifeline thrown to save a soul sinking into the abyss of addiction. This chapter delves into the emotional maelstrom of that intervention, the courageous attempt by her inner circle to rescue her from the grip of self-destruction.

As Amy's struggles with addiction escalated, her once-dazzling star became increasingly dimmed. The demons of drugs and alcohol had claimed her, and her downward spiral was heart-wrenching to witness. Friends and family, their hearts heavy with worry and love, understood that complacency would equate to complicity in her potential demise. It was time to act.

The intervention was a gathering of souls who had watched her light flicker, yet refused to let it be extinguished. It was a tableau of raw emotion, marked by tears, anguish, and unwavering determination. Those who loved Amy knew that they were fighting not only for her career but for her very life. The price of inaction was too catastrophic to contemplate.

Amy's response to the intervention was a tempest of emotions. The independent spirit that had defined her collided with anger and denial, giving way, at times, to a reluctant acceptance. She was a soul torn between rebellion and the glimmer of recognition that perhaps, just perhaps, this was the lifeline she so desperately needed.

The decision to enter rehab was a courageous step, a sign that Amy had not completely surrendered to the darkness that had consumed her. It was a glimmer of hope for her fans and a testament to the love and support of those who refused to give up on her. The world watched with a mix of hope and trepidation as she embarked on this arduous journey of rehabilitation.

Rehabilitation was not a silver bullet; it was a battle on multiple fronts. Amy had to grapple with the physical and psychological dependencies that had held her captive. Detoxification was a painful ordeal, and the emotional wounds ran deep. It was the unwavering love of her inner circle and the guidance of professionals that became her pillars of strength.

Throughout her rehabilitation, music was her sanctuary. In the midst of the struggle, Amy found solace in her art. The songs that emerged during this period were poignant, bearing witness to the pain and vulnerability of her journey. They were not just lyrics and melodies; they were the emotional scars she willingly bared for the world to see.

Emerging from rehab, Amy faced a daunting road to recovery. The paparazzi, always in pursuit of a story, continued to hound her. The world watched with bated breath, hoping for her triumphant return, but ever vigilant for signs of relapse. The emotional toll of her battle was etched in every line of her face, and yet, there was a glimmer of resilience in her eyes.

"Chapter Fifteen: The Intervention and Rehab" peels back the layers of this poignant chapter in Amy Winehouse's life. It reveals the depths of love and concern that led to the intervention, laying bare the raw emotions of both Amy and her loved ones. It delves into the challenges of rehabilitation, the painful process of recovery, and the unrelenting gaze of the public and the paparazzi. Amidst the tumult, Amy's music remained a powerful testimony to her indomitable spirit and her unwavering determination to defy the odds.

Chapter Sixteen: The Troubled Return

Amy Winehouse's journey back into the world after rehab was a deeply complex and turbulent period in her life. This chapter unearths the intricate details of her troubled return, a time characterized by the fragility of recovery and the ever-present shadow of relapse.

As Amy gingerly re-emerged into the world, she carried with her a newfound determination to conquer her addiction demons. She had stared into the abyss and now yearned for a return to the days when her music, not her struggles, defined her. However, the world, with its skeptical eyes, remained wary, and the relentless paparazzi continued their relentless pursuit of headlines.

The tempestuous relationship with her ex-husband, Blake Fielder-Civil, remained an enigmatic and often painful undercurrent in her life. Their connection was marked by a rollercoaster of emotions, an intricate dance of passion and despair that the public observed with a mix of fascination and concern.

Amy's battle with addiction persisted as a daily challenge. The allure of her old habits and the relentless temptations were a constant reminder of the fragility of her recovery. It was the unwavering support and love of her inner circle that acted as a lifeline, but the siren call of her past remained a formidable adversary.

Yet, amidst the chaos and uncertainty, Amy's music continued to be her guiding light. She poured her experiences, her pain, and her quest for redemption into her songs. Each lyric was a testament to her unwavering determination, and each note became a proclamation of her indomitable spirit.

The Troubled Return was not merely a chapter in Amy's life; it was a testament to the extraordinary resilience of the human spirit. It was a narrative of hope and strife, of love and vulnerability. Amy's return was a journey through a tempest, and the world watched, holding its breath, with the fervent hope that she would find her way back to the music and the life that had once been her true north.

"Chapter Sixteen: The Troubled Return" is an immersive exploration of this tumultuous period in Amy Winehouse's life. It unveils the intricate dynamics of recovery's fragility and the omnipresent specter of relapse. It delves into the intricacies of her relationship with Blake Fielder-Civil and the daily grapple with addiction's relentless pull. Through it all, her music emerges as a powerful testament to her unyielding spirit, a guiding star in the darkest of nights.

Chapter Sixteen: The Troubled Return

In the intricate tapestry of Amy Winehouse's life, the chapter titled "The Troubled Return" stands as a testament to the indomitable human spirit, the battle between darkness and light, and the complexities of recovery. It's a story of resilience, vulnerability, and a longing for redemption that resonated in every lyric she penned.

Amy's re-entry into the world after rehab was a delicate dance on the precipice of hope and despair. It was a period marked by the fragility of recovery, the ever-present shadow of relapse, and the collective yearning for her triumphant return. The world watched, holding its breath, as she took her first steps on this perilous path.

The relationship with her ex-husband, Blake Fielder-Civil, remained the enigmatic heartbeat of her life. It was a complex and tempestuous connection, a love story that had captivated the public's imagination. Their tumultuous bond was a narrative of passion and despair, a rollercoaster of emotions that veered between euphoria and heartbreak. The world observed their dance with a mix of fascination and concern, hoping that love would conquer all.

Amy's struggle with addiction was far from over; it was an unrelenting companion that shadowed her every move. The siren call of old habits and the constant temptations were a reminder of the fragility of her recovery. The battles were fought daily, and the scars were etched into her soul. Yet, amidst the ongoing war with her demons, there was a fierce determination to overcome.

The return to a world that had watched her descent was marked by both hope and skepticism. The paparazzi remained a relentless presence, eager for the next headline, the next fall from grace. Amy's every move was scrutinized, her every action fodder for tabloids. It was a reminder of the unforgiving nature of fame.

Throughout this tumultuous period, Amy's music remained her sanctuary, her refuge from the chaos. Her songs were not just art; they were her emotional landscape. She channeled her experiences, her pain, and her yearning for redemption into every lyric. Each word was a raw confession, and each note a testament to her unwavering spirit.

"The Troubled Return" was not just a chapter in Amy's life; it was a profound exploration of the human spirit's capacity for renewal. It was a narrative of hope and resilience, of love and vulnerability, and of an unyielding longing for redemption. Amy's journey was an odyssey through the tempest, and the world watched, collectively holding its breath, hoping that she would rediscover her place in music and in life.

In "Chapter Sixteen: The Troubled Return," we embark on a detailed and emotional journey through this tumultuous phase in Amy Winehouse's life. We delve into the intricacies of her fragile recovery, the ever-present specter of relapse, and the complexities of her relationship with Blake Fielder-Civil. Through it all, her music emerges as a powerful testament to her unyielding spirit, a guiding star in the darkest of nights.

Chapter Eighteen: Legacy and Posthumous Recognition

The world was left in mourning when the news of Amy Winehouse's untimely passing shook the music industry and touched the hearts of her fans across the globe. But beyond the profound grief, Amy's legacy continued to shine brightly, a beacon of her remarkable talent and the enduring impact she had on the world of music.

Amy's death at the tender age of 27 was a devastating reminder of the perils of addiction. It was a tragic end to a life that had once blazed with the brilliance of her unique talent. Her fans, friends, and family were left grappling with the cruel reality of a world without her voice.

Yet, in the wake of her passing, something extraordinary happened. Amy's music, which had always been powerful, experienced a resurgence of popularity. Her albums, from the heart-wrenching "Back to Black" to her debut "Frank," climbed the charts once more. A new generation discovered the timeless quality of her work, each note a raw emotion, and each lyric a window into her soul.

But Amy's legacy wasn't just about chart-topping albums. It was about the indelible mark she had left on the very fabric of the music industry. Her genre-defying blend of jazz, soul, and R&B had broken new ground, paving the way for a resurgence of interest in these classic genres. Artists across the globe found inspiration in her unconventional approach to music, her candid storytelling, and her fearless vulnerability.

Beyond the music, Amy's iconic fashion sense had left an indelible mark. The beehive hair and winged eyeliner became synonymous with her name. Her look, a blend of vintage elegance and contemporary edge, resonated with fans and fashion enthusiasts alike. It was a style that reflected her timeless artistry and her unapologetic individuality.

Amy's legacy also transcended into the realm of compassion. Her family, led by her parents Janis and Mitch Winehouse, established the Amy Winehouse Foundation. This charitable organization aimed to support young people facing addiction and other life challenges. It was a way for the Winehouse family to channel Amy's spirit of resilience and compassion into meaningful change, offering hope to countless individuals.

Posthumously, Amy continued to receive accolades and recognition for her contributions to music. Awards and honors, including Grammy Awards and Brit Awards, celebrated her enduring influence on the industry. Her music found its way into films, documentaries, and commercials, introducing her voice to new audiences and ensuring her memory remained vivid.

Despite her tragic end, Amy's legacy lived on. It lived in the timeless quality of her music, in her influence on the industry, and in the charitable efforts of her family. Amy Winehouse's name remained etched in the annals of music history, a poignant reminder of the profound connection she had formed with her listeners and the enduring impact of her artistry.

"Chapter Eighteen: Legacy and Posthumous Recognition" is a heartfelt reflection on the lasting imprint of Amy Winehouse. It delves into the resurgence of her music, her influence on the industry, and the charitable efforts of her family. Her legacy, shaped by her unique style and timeless music, continues to inspire new generations, serving as a poignant reminder of the incredible talent and the profound struggles that defined her life. It's a tribute to a remarkable artist whose memory lives on in the hearts of those who loved her.

Chapter Nineteen: Amy's Influence on Music

As we delve into the rich tapestry of Amy Winehouse's life, we encounter a chapter that transcends the boundaries of her own story, for it's a chapter that chronicles her profound influence on the world of music—a legacy that continues to resonate, even in her absence.

Amy was a musical force of nature, an artist whose evocative voice and unapologetic storytelling breathed new life into genres that had long slumbered. Her unique blend of jazz, soul, and R&B wasn't just a genre; it was an emotional landscape she fearlessly navigated. In a world dominated by cookie-cutter pop, Amy's music was a defiant call to authenticity.

Her signature album, "Back to Black," was a masterpiece that redefined modern soul music. Its raw, confessional lyrics and melancholic melodies cut through the airwaves with a piercing clarity. The album was a declaration of pain and resilience, a testament to the power of vulnerability in music. It resonated deeply with fans who found solace in her unfiltered honesty.

But it wasn't just her chart-topping albums that set her apart; it was the courage to sing about the unspoken, the messy, and the real. Amy's lyrics were a window into her tumultuous life—love, heartbreak, addiction, and redemption. Each song was a chapter in her life's book, laid bare for the world to see.

Her fearless storytelling, marked by a candid exploration of addiction and the dark recesses of her soul, ignited a revolution in songwriting. Her songs didn't sugarcoat reality; they embraced it with all its imperfections. The world of music was forever changed, as artists from various genres began to infuse their work with the same unfiltered vulnerability that had become synonymous with Amy's name.

Amy's influence extended far beyond her genre, transcending borders and resonating with artists around the world. She had rekindled the love for jazz, soul, and R&B, ushering in a revival of these classic genres. Her music was a bridge between the past and the present, a reminder of the enduring power of timeless melodies and genuine emotion.

The impact of Amy's work wasn't confined to her lifetime. Even after her untimely passing, her music continued to inspire and shape the industry. Her influence was evident in the artistry of those who admired her, from Adele to Bruno Mars, who carried forward the torch of soulful, authentic storytelling. They had learned from the best—the incomparable Amy Winehouse.

But her legacy wasn't limited to just sound. Amy's iconic fashion sense, with the beehive hair and winged eyeliner, influenced style trends across the globe. Her look was a blend of vintage elegance and contemporary edge, a reflection of her timeless artistry and her unapologetic individuality. Fashion enthusiasts and fans alike sought to capture her unique style.

Beyond the realm of music and fashion, Amy's family, led by her parents Janis and Mitch Winehouse, established the Amy Winehouse Foundation. This charitable organization aimed to support young people facing addiction and other life challenges. It was a way for the Winehouse family to channel Amy's spirit of resilience and compassion into meaningful change, offering hope to countless individuals.

"Chapter Nineteen: Amy's Influence on Music" is a heartfelt exploration of the profound impact Amy Winehouse had on the world of music. It delves into her fearless storytelling, her revival of classic genres, and her influence on artists both young and established. Amy's legacy continues to shape the industry, serving as a reminder that authenticity and vulnerability in music can touch the deepest corners of the human heart. It's a tribute to an artist whose influence refuses to be confined to her time but lives on in the melodies and stories she left behind.

Conclusion

In the tapestry of Amy Winehouse's life, one finds a story that transcends the boundaries of music, fame, and the public eye. It is a story of extraordinary talent, unyielding passion, and profound vulnerability. Her life was a journey marked by dazzling highs and crushing lows, but it was also a journey that resonated with countless souls around the world.

Amy's music, with its genre-defying blend of jazz, soul, and R&B, was a force of nature. It defied convention and struck a chord deep within the hearts of listeners. Her albums, especially the iconic "Back to Black," remain timeless classics. They are more than just collections of songs; they are emotional landscapes, raw and unfiltered. Amy's lyrics were confessions, each note a vivid expression of her tumultuous life.

But it was her willingness to sing about the unspoken, the messy, and the real that set her apart.

Her songs were a mirror to her struggles and her triumphs, her addictions, and her journey toward redemption. It was this honesty that revolutionized the world of songwriting. Her influence was a catalyst for artists from various genres who found inspiration in her unapologetic vulnerability.

Amy's impact extended far beyond music. Her fashion sense, featuring the iconic beehive hair and winged eyeliner, became synonymous with her unique style. It was a look that defied trends and became a symbol of her timeless individuality. Her influence was felt not only in music but also on the runway and in the hearts of fashion enthusiasts.

The legacy she left wasn't limited to sound or style; it was a legacy of compassion. Her family, led by her parents Janis and Mitch Winehouse, founded the Amy Winehouse Foundation. This charitable organization was a beacon of hope for young people facing addiction and life challenges. It embodied the spirit of resilience and compassion that Amy had shown throughout her life.

Amy's untimely passing was a tragic reminder of the devastating consequences of addiction. It was a reminder of the fragility of life and the unrelenting grip of addiction. But her legacy, her music, and her influence live on. They are a testament to the enduring power of art, the authenticity of vulnerability, and the boundless reach of compassion.

In the end, Amy Winehouse's life was a masterpiece, much like her music. It was a composition of brilliance and tumult, a symphony of highs and lows. Her story was a reminder that even in the depths of darkness, there can be redemption, and even in the midst of vulnerability, there can be strength. She was more than a singer; she was a storyteller, and her stories will continue to resonate with generations to come.

In this biography, we've explored the life of Amy Winehouse, from her troubled childhood to her meteoric rise to fame, her battles with addiction, her triumphant return, and her enduring legacy. It's a story of a woman who lived passionately, sang fearlessly, and left an indelible mark on the world. Amy Winehouse's journey was one of rehab to redemption, and her story will continue to inspire and touch the hearts of all who listen.

Printed in Great Britain
by Amazon